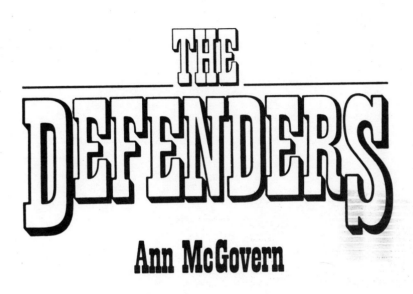

THE DEFENDERS

Ann McGovern

SCHOLASTIC INC.
New York Toronto London Auckland Sydney

Photo Acknowledgments

Courtesy of The American Museum of Natural History: pp. 47, 95;
Courtesy of Associated Press and *The New York Times:* p. 48; Bett-
man Archive: pp. 76, 79, 92, 101; *Harper's:* pp. 109, 118, 121 (right),
123; Library of Congress: pp. 32, 38, 75; Harry T. Peters Collection,
Museum of the City of New York: p. 58; National Archives: pp. 114,
126; Negro History Associates: p. 15 (right); Courtesy of the New
York Historical Society: p. 15 (left); New York Public Library Pic-
ture Collection: pp. 53, 63, 86, 121 (left); Smithsonian Institution:
p. 50; Whipple Collection, Oklahoma Historical Society: p. 84; U.S.
Bureau of Ethnology: p. 17.

ISBN 0-590-43866-2

22   23/0

Printed in the U.S.A.   40

THE DEFENDERS tells the exciting and tragic stories of three great Indian leaders,who fought bravely for their people's freedom and their right to live on their own lands. The battles took place in the Florida swamps, in the Midwest, and on the Western Plains, at a time when our nation was expanding rapidly. Lands were seized and thousands of people were killed or made captive in the name of progress.

These stories are a part of the long struggle for human liberty in our country—as well as tragic chapters in the history of the first Americans.

How to say these Indian names:

Algonquian (tribal nation or language)	Al-GON-kwee-in
Aravaipa (an Apache tribe)	Ah-rah-VĪ-pa
Apache (tribal nation or language)	Uh-PATCH-ee
Chiricahua (Apache tribe to which Cochise belonged)	Chir-ic-KOW-wa
Cochise (Apache chief)	Co-CHEEZ
Coyotero (an Apache tribe)	Kī-oh-TARE-oh
Laulewasika (Tecumseh's youngest brother)	Law-lee-WA-sick-ah
Micanopy (Head chief of the Seminoles)	Mi-kun-NO-pea
Osceola (Seminole chief)	Ah-see-OH-la
Seminole (tribal nation or language)	SEM-in-ole
Shawnee (tribal nation or language)	Shaw-NEE
Tecumseh (Shawnee chief)	Teh-KUM-seh

Contents

Osceola

1 "Seize Him!"

O SCEOLA kept his dark eyes on the face of General Wiley Thompson.

The general was speaking — earnestly, a little impatiently — to the Seminole leaders he had called together.

He was saying, "Fine fertile lands await you in the western country. Good hunting grounds you can keep forever. The United States will give you seeds, tools, money."

The Seminoles had heard these words before. They were words of promise. Treaty words. Thompson had called this council to get the Seminoles to sign another treaty. A treaty that would send them from their Florida homeland forever.

A Seminole named Osceola was present at this

Osceola.
A painting by George Catlin.

council. He was not a chief, not even a lesser chief. Yet in this year 1834, Micanopy, the principal chief of the Florida Seminoles, looked to him as a leader.

Osceola too had heard Thompson's promises before. And now his thoughts were bitter. "The white man wants our groves of orange trees, our fine harbors, our full forests, and warm fertile lands. But they are ours. Here are our fish and birds and animals, the graves of our fathers, the grounds of our children."

He looked around at the silent chiefs and wondered which of them would speak.

Then, one by one General Thompson called the chiefs to come forward to sign the treaty.

Four chiefs refused.

General Thompson lost his temper. "You are no longer chiefs," he shouted at them. "The Americans will not recognize you as leaders of your people."

Osceola walked boldly to the table.

Eagerly, General Thompson pushed the quill pen toward him. Osceola did not look at it. Instead, he drew out his hunting knife. Then he plunged the knife into the treaty paper, pinning it to the rough pine table. "This," he said, "is the only treaty I make with the whites."

"Seize him!" General Thompson thundered. It took four soldiers to subdue Osceola. They put him in irons and threw him into prison.

Osceola was told, "Only when you agree to sign the treaty will you be released."

2 A Terrible Treaty

LOCKED in the dark prison, Osceola's thoughts were bitter.

He knew what a terrible treaty he was being asked to sign. It was not only Seminole land that the white men wanted. They wanted the Seminoles whose skins were black. For the treaty had this to say: *No Seminole who had Negro blood could go to the western country.*

How this would tear brother from brother! Wife would be taken from husband. Child would be torn from parents. For among the Seminoles the black man and the red man had lived together now for a long, long time. The blood of many of them ran together through the children of many marriages.

Some of the blacks among the Seminoles had been born free. Others had run away from slavery on plantations in the United States. They had fled to the forests and swamps of Florida. There, the runaways had settled among the free blacks and in the Seminole villages.

The Seminoles befriended the runaways. They taught the blacks how to carve cypress canoes and how to make bread from the coontie plant. The blacks taught the Seminoles better ways of farming.

Now who could tell if a black man had been born free, or his freedom bought from a white man, or if he was the grandson of a Seminole chief? And what did it matter? Through the years the black men and the red men had become part of one tribe, one Seminole Nation.

But the slave catchers never gave up. No Seminole was really safe. In treaty after treaty the Seminoles had been promised that *this time* white men would not be allowed to hunt or settle or intrude upon their land. Still white men crossed the Seminole borders. They raided villages, stole cattle, destroyed crops. And they seized black Seminoles as slaves.

In 1817, what is now known as the First Seminole War started when an American general sent his men across the Spanish border into Florida to arrest a Seminole chief accused of sheltering escaped slaves. The slave owners had long wanted the U.S. to take the Florida territory from Spain. And by February 1819, it was done. The war was over; Spain had been defeated. Florida belonged to the U.S.

And ever since, the whites had been pressing harder and harder. Get the Seminoles out to the West! But not the black Seminoles. They were worth a fortune as slaves.

Micanopy. Head Chief of the Seminoles.

Abraham. A black Seminole who served as translator for the Seminole chiefs.

Now General Thompson was asking Osceola to sign a treaty that would send the Seminoles from their homeland and deliver his black brothers into the hands of the slave owners.

How could he sign such a treaty?

But only if he signed would he be released from prison.

"Very well," thought Osceola. "I will use the white man's trickery. I will sign this white man's treaty so I can leave his prison. But I will never give up our land or betray our brothers. Instead, I will make the white man red with blood and then blacken him in the sun and rain, where the wolf shall smell of his bones and the buzzards shall live on his flesh."

3 Osceola Learns

OSCEOLA did not talk lightly of war or of killing. He never forgot what his mother had taught him: Do not take a life unless your own is in danger.

He knew too what war would mean for his people, the suffering it would bring. In war time they would have to leave their *chickees* — their thatched log houses — to live in the marshy, murky swamps.

They could not build their eating houses, where there was always a *sofkee* kettle bubbling with a turtle steak or a juicy venison or fish stew. In war time, whatever fish they could catch they would eat raw.

And no longer would his people be able to sit gazing for hours into a fire smelling of the rich pitch pine. In war time there must be no fires for the enemy to see.

Osceola knew well the hardships of war, for he had spent much of his childhood in such a time.

War had forced Osceola and his mother to flee the land of Georgia, where, in 1804, Osceola was born. When he was a child, he and his mother had been taken prisoners during the First Seminole War. When they were freed, they wandered south until at last they came to Florida, the only home Osceola really knew.

In his Florida home Osceola learned early how to live as a wanderer. He learned to move swiftly and with grace. From the time he was a boy, the other Seminoles called him a bold hunter and a fine fisherman. His bright arrows always found their mark.

A Seminole chickee. Because of the warm climate, the house is open on all sides. The floor is raised from the muddy ground. And the roof, made of thatched palmetto leaves, makes an umbrella against sun and rain.

And few could spear so well the small silver fish in the lake.

Osceola learned the names of plants and creatures. He learned which berries and nuts and fruits could be eaten and which ones were poisonous. He learned how to make a cup from a leaf to drink the clear Florida water.

Osceola learned to endure hardship. He grew used to the night cold, the biting mosquito, the cries of wild animals.

He grew to manhood without fear. He grew to manhood as a Seminole.

Now, as a man, what Osceola could not grow used to was the way white men felt about Indians. To Osceola it seemed that most white men looked upon the Indian as a creature without human feelings — to be tricked, to be cheated, to be destroyed.

Now a white man was asking him, Osceola, to betray his people.

"They want me to sign their treaty," he thought. "Very well, let the Indian learn to lie as the white man lies."

Osceola signed the treaty. For he needed to be free in the days ahead.

Free to fight.

4 "The Spirit of War"

Sixteen chiefs also signed the treaty. "It is no use trying to fight the mighty forces of the white man," they said. "We must prepare to leave our homes."

General Wiley Thompson ordered the Seminole chiefs to bring their people to Tampa Bay by January 15, 1835, the following year. There, transport boats would be waiting to take them away.

Osceola had signed the hated treaty too. But he did not intend to give up the land. And he tried again and again to strengthen the will of the other leaders.

"True, we are a weak nation," he told them. "Our people number only four thousand. We have perhaps only fifteen hundred warriors. The white man has many thousand soldiers. His nation is strong. Yet I say we must fight this war. We must use the cunning of the fox, the swiftness of the snake, to fight the wolves!"

Those chiefs who had agreed to leave were nevertheless fearful. For one thing, they were afraid of old enemy tribes awaiting them in the West.

They appealed to General Thompson for special protection in their new home. Thompson sent their request to the U.S. government in Washington. The answer came back a few weeks later. Their wish would not be granted.

"Is it not clearer now than ever?" Osceola cried. "The white men will never help us!"

He begged the principal chief, Micanopy, to call a council of war. This Micanopy did.

Osceola's words at the council gave strength to the weak but they struck fear into those who would still go West.

"I say our homes and our land must be saved at any cost," Osceola said. "To the cowards I say: You wish to go West. You wish to sell your property, your cattle? Listen well. If one of you so much as gets rid of one horse, one pony, one chicken, you are a traitor! And you will die."

Frightened by these threats, five of the chiefs who had signed the treaty gathered their followers and fled to Tampa Bay. There they asked the army to protect them.

General Thompson began to worry. He could no longer ignore the signs of war.

More and more Seminoles were leaving their faraway villages to join Osceola. Women and children

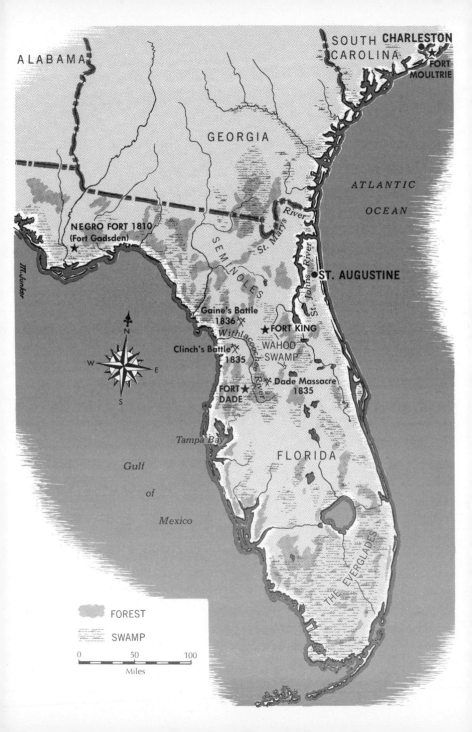

were disappearing from their villages, sent to hide in the shelter of the swamps.

Now General Thompson gave the orders to the white traders: "No more rifles and bullets to the Indians."

His orders were not obeyed. There was a lot of money to be made selling guns to the Indians. And the Seminoles were willing to trade anything of value to get arms. They piled up more and more weapons.

There was another sign of the growing unrest. The news of what happened to Chief Charley Emanthla spread through Florida like wildfire.

Chief Emanthla favored removal to the West. One day he paid a visit to the whites to arrange protection for the departure of his tribe and to sell his cattle. The gold and silver he had been paid was wrapped safely in his handkerchief.

He started back to his village. But he never reached his chickee.

Osceola and twelve Seminoles lay hidden behind thick trees, waiting. When Chief Emanthla approached, they stepped out into the clearing.

"You have agreed to deliver your people to the whites to be sent West," Osceola accused him. "You have sold the cattle of your people to the white man for gold and silver. You are a traitor to your people. You know the penalty."

Osceola raised his rifle and fired.

Then he bent down and removed from Chief

Emanthla's body the handkerchief filled with gold and silver coins. He threw the coins as far as he could, scattering them in every direction. "Let no one touch them," Osceola said.

To his enemies, Osceola was a fierce and cunning foe. To his people he was a great patriot. They called him "the Spirit of War." To his wives and children, he was a kind and gentle husband and father. It was the custom of the Seminole Indians to take two wives. Osceola loved both of his wives dearly.

One day he came to the trading post at Fort King where General Thompson was in command. With him were several companions and the younger of his wives. Her name in Seminole was Che-Co-Ter. The white men called her Morning Dew. Her father was a Seminole chief. Because her mother was a black woman, in the eyes of the white man Morning Dew was a slave.

Osceola was inside the fort talking with General Thompson when he heard a scream. He rushed outside the fort and saw Morning Dew being carried away by slave catchers.

"She is my wife," he shouted to Thompson. "Save her."

But General Thompson did nothing. Osceola was filled with a rage so wild that Thompson had him locked in irons. Wildly, madly, Osceola struggled to free himself. But the more he struggled, the more the irons cut deeply into his flesh. Helplessly he watched the white men steal his wife.

Thompson soon realized that locking Osceola up was a mistake. The Seminoles were angered. And because there was no reason to keep Osceola in jail, Thompson had to release him.

Silently, Osceola left the jail. Swiftly, he mounted his horse and rode toward his village. Then above the sound of the galloping hooves, General Thompson heard Osceola's chilling cry: *"Yo-ho-e-he!"*

It was the Seminole war cry.

5 The War Begins

O SCEOLA's cry was not only a call to battle.

It was also a personal message to General Thompson. For Osceola did not intend to let the kidnaping of his wife go unavenged.

Osceola began to study every movement that General Thompson made. Soon he knew that regularly the general went to dine with a friend, that regularly he took the same path back to the fort.

On the morning of December 28th, General Thompson was walking as usual. But this time Osceola and a war party were waiting.

It was Osceola who struck down the general. And it was the Seminole war cry — *Yo-ho-e-he!* that General Thompson heard as he fell dead.

Word now reached Osceola that American troops under the command of a Major Dade were marching north from Tampa Bay to reinforce Fort King.

This was what the Seminoles had long waited for — the chance to trap the enemy where they could not fight from the protection of a fort. Osceola and his warriors hurried south toward the Big Wahoo Swamp.

By the time Osceola arrived, the battle had been fought and won by the Seminoles. It had been a disaster for Dade and his men.

Many times Osceola had told his warriors: "Show mercy. Act like men." Now the victorious Seminoles took all the ammunition they could lay their hands on. But they did not take a single scalp.

There was a victory celebration at the Big Wahoo Swamp which lasted three days. Then scouts came hurrying to the swamp with word that another army was approaching, this time led by General Clinch. There were many men, the scouts said — nearly eight hundred!

By the time General Clinch arrived with his army, not a Seminole was to be seen. The only sign of their presence was a canoe, lying on its side in the water. General Clinch seized the canoe and put it to use ferrying his men to the other side of the Withlacoochee River.

About two hundred and fifty of the soldiers had reached the other side of the river, when suddenly the Seminoles rose from their hiding places and attacked. The general's army was now split in two. The five hundred men who were unable to cross the river watched helplessly as their comrades and the

Seminoles fired at each other through the dense swamp grass.

Three times that day, General Clinch ordered his men into combat with fixed bayonet. Then as they continued to fall before the Seminoles' fire, he called retreat.

The news flew like Osceola's swiftest arrow. Dead! General Thompson. Dead! Major Dade and one hundred of his men. General Clinch, in retreat. All within three days!

Osceola was keeping his promise — "I will make the white man red with blood."

6 A Season of Fear

"CAPTURE every Seminole in Florida!" President Andrew Jackson ordered.

It was one thing to give orders from a government building in Washington. It was quite another thing to carry them out in the swamps of Florida.

Every Seminole was fighting this war to save his home and his people. Old men and women, and boys and girls too young to hold a rifle, all were doing their part. They made bullets. They stored supplies. They cooked for the fighting warriors.

Now another general was called in to direct the war, General Edmund Gaines. His plan was to take a stand on the banks of the Withlacoochee River. But when his men reached the river, they found themselves surrounded by Seminoles. The general's scouts reported that there were at least fourteen hundred. For days the soldiers were hemmed in, unable to cross the river.

In the night they could see the Seminole campfires and hear the war cries of the warriors. Once General Gaines even caught a glimpse of Osceola, his face and body painted in the Seminole colors of war.

In desperation, Gaines sent a messenger to General Clinch. Somehow the man got through the tight Seminole lines and reached General Clinch. The message said: send more troops immediately!

A week went by. Still Gaines waited for help. His men grew hungrier and hungrier. A little corn was all they had left. Soon the soldiers began to kill their horses for food.

One day a man came to Gaines's camp with a message from Osceola. He wished to discuss peace. He wished to have a council. Eagerly Gaines agreed.

Speaking at the council, Osceola said, "Our people are tired of fighting. We have lost many warriors. We wish for peace."

The general was also eager to have peace. He and the Seminole leaders began to discuss the terms on which the fighting could stop. Unfortunately, it was at this moment that General Clinch and the advance guard of his troops arrived.

General Clinch had marched his army north and south, looking for the elusive Seminoles. His men were hot and tired and angry. They came to the Withlacoochee River and here at last there were Indians. They fired.

Three Seminoles were killed. The rest of the Seminoles fled into the woods. They were sure they had been tricked again. Tricked at a peace council.

By nightfall, not one Seminole could be seen. Without a sign, without a sound, they had disappeared — more than a thousand of them — into the deepest shadows of the swamps.

Another general was called in to take command — General Winfield Scott. General Scott collected the largest army yet gathered in Florida.

He divided his men into three columns. His soldiers kept each other informed of their whereabouts by firing their cannon as signals.

Osceola and his warriors had to laugh at this. Did the white soldiers think that the Seminoles were born without ears? The bursts of cannon fire told them exactly where their enemy was at all times.

General Scott's men also searched in vain for the Seminoles' hiding places. These soldiers too were not used to this way of fighting a war. They were used to shelters, to open roads, to fighting the enemy face to face.

But this miserable country was without roads, without forts. Here the enemy remained hidden in secret marshland places.

The white soldiers found this maddening and frightening. What kind of fighting was this? They couldn't even *see* the enemy. They traded shots with shadows in a thicket of cypress. The Seminoles seemed to attack from nowhere. In small bands, they emerged from their hidden places in swamps and grasses, attacking swiftly, striking suddenly at the rear of the marching troops, then disappearing once again.

In the same terrifying way, the Seminoles attacked army posts and settlements.

All that winter the frontier was aflame. The people of Florida slept restlessly. Who could tell when a cabin or a barn would suddenly be set on fire?

Would they wake to see a band of armed Indians at their window?

It was a season of fear.

Then it was spring. And, for the Seminoles, it was a season of hunger. There had been no time to plant corn or to hunt game in the forest. Their cattle had long since been taken by the whites.

Sometimes the warriors told their women and children to stay hidden in the swamps. They dared not then come out to hunt or fish. Sometimes the women and children went hungry for hours, even days, shivering in their wet, cold clothes.

They longed for their homes, their villages, their cornfields and gardens in their light, bright, sunlit world. Now their homes were the dark swamps where wild, tangled greens hid them from enemy eyes.

Sometimes, from the swamps where they lay hidden they could hear the enemy coming close. Then

quickly the Seminole women would bury their children in pits they had dug. They would cover the children's faces with palm leaves and warn them softly not to cry out. Only when their children were safe, would they look to themselves. Then they hid in the water, covering their faces with lily pads.

Yet great as their suffering was, the Seminoles would not give up.

General Scott was called to Washington. President Jackson was furious that he had not ended the war. And a new general got his orders. General Call.

General Call acted quickly. He sent for bloodhounds. "If soldiers can't track down the Seminoles, surely dogs will!"

The newspaper in St. Augustine, Florida, reported: "We hope soon to hear they are on the scent of the enemy."

But it was not a war that could be won with dogs.

General Call's soldiers came to the jungle, the forest, and the swamp. They came sweating in the heat, cursing and dragging their guns.

They did not know, as the Seminoles did, how to avoid the bogs where the deadly moccasin snake

An attack by Seminoles on a U.S. blockhouse. The blockhouse is a small two-story structure made of heavy timbers. The sides are pierced with holes from which men fired on attackers. The top story was often used as an observation post.

slithered, or the forest where the diamondback rattler sounded its death warning. They learned — often too late — that the alligator was not the peaceful drifting log it seemed to be. At night the air thickened with mosquitoes. Who could sleep with their constant biting and swarming?

General Call's men died as often from the bite of the snake and the mosquito as they did from the weapons of the Seminoles.

In the wet summer months, disease came to the swamps. In June and July, malaria fever killed many Seminoles. The fever did not spare even the "Spirit of the War." Osceola too was stricken.

Malaria killed hundreds of U.S. soldiers and weakened hundreds more. In Washington, General Call's efforts to win the war had to be written down as another failure.

7 The Promise Is Broken

THE SEMINOLE WAR had to end. But how? Give Florida back to the Seminoles? Never! Then get the Seminoles out of Florida. Yes! — but how? General after general had failed.

There was only one answer to this whole Seminole problem, said the government men. Osceola! Wasn't he the great "Spirit of the War"? Kill the Spirit of the War and end the war!

General Thomas Jesup was called in.

He was determined to do what other generals had failed to do. *He would win this war.* And he would capture Osceola.

Jesup was a cautious man. He went over his plans carefully. He would avoid sending large numbers of soldiers into the deadly swamps. He would make sure to have enough supplies.

He called upon the old enemy of the Seminoles, the Creeks, to join him in battle. He promised the

Creeks that they could take black Seminoles as prisoners — and then they could sell them as slaves.

He put his plans to work.

The soldiers and the Creeks entered the swamps and began their attack.

First sixteen black Seminoles were captured. Then thirty-six more. Then cattle and horses, ammunition and supplies. Then twenty-five more Seminoles — mostly women and children.

But what of Osceola? With each day that passed, General Jesup could think of little else. Where was he?

Finally General Jesup sent a message to the Seminoles. The message offered peace if they would get out of Florida.

Once more, the chiefs agreed to meet. In his official report to the government, the general wrote: "I shall probably be able to follow the enemy into their most hidden retreats, should they reject the terms offered them."

The meeting took place but Osceola was not there. The chiefs listened to the offer of peace. They must leave Florida. They had heard these words before.

Then suddenly, General Jesup was saying something new, something wonderfully different.

The black Seminoles would be allowed to go West with the Nation. Furthermore, Jesup said that the government would pay the Seminoles a fair price for their cattle and ponies. He promised that "all would be secure in their lives and property."

The chiefs heard the offer with joy. After all these years, the rights of the black Seminoles were going to be protected.

The chiefs agreed to this. They would gather their people together for the journey West.

When Osceola heard, he too agreed. But did the United States government really mean to carry out the promises that General Jesup had made? Most important was the promise that their black brothers could go in safety to the West.

The Seminoles began coming together at Tampa Bay. There, drifting at anchor, were the twenty-six boats waiting to move them on the first lap of their journey.

General Jesup was sure now that at last the war was over. But he had made his plans without the slave catchers.

They too began gathering at Tampa Bay. When he learned of this, Jesup was angry. He wrote to the officer in command at Tampa Bay and ordered the slave owners to leave. The Seminoles did not wish to war again, he said, but any attempt to seize black Seminoles "would be followed by an instant resort to arms."

But to the slave owner, the main purpose of this Second Seminole War was to capture the black Seminoles. When the slave owners heard that General Jesup had agreed to let black Seminoles go West, they raised a storm of protest. They went to Washington and said, "To end the war on such terms

would be a clear triumph on the part of the Indian."

Jesup could not stand up against the slave owners and their powerful friends in the government. He gave in to their demands. He would try something else. "I have hopes," he wrote, "of inducing both Indians and Indian Negroes to unite in bringing in the Negroes taken from the citizens during the war."

But who could tell which Negro had run away, or which Negro had always lived with his Seminole Nation?

The slave catchers could not tell and it was clear they did not care. They swarmed into the Tampa Bay area and seized anyone with a black skin.

With Osceola in charge, all the Seminoles fled for their lives. One night, more than seven hundred chiefs, warriors, and their families disappeared into the safety of the swamps. And as they fled, they warned all others who were still planning to come to Tampa Bay, to save themselves.

Newspapers all over the United States blamed Jesup for letting the Seminoles slip through his grasp — especially Osceola.

The general had all of this war he could take. He asked permission to return to Washington. His request was turned down. To the Secretary of War he wrote: "To rid the country of them you must exterminate them. Is the government prepared for such a measure? Will public opinion sustain it?"

American camp at Tampa Bay, Florida.

Seminole Indians of the Florida Everglades, wearing their national dress.

Then he wrote to a fellow officer in the army: "If you see Osceola again, tell him that I intend to send exploring parties into every part of the country this summer. I shall send out and take all the Negroes who belong to the white people, and he must not allow the Indians or the Indian Negroes to mix with them. Tell him I am sending for bloodhounds to trail them and I intend to hang everyone of them who does not come in."

Jesup also wrote to commanding officers at several army posts in Seminole territory. He told the military officers that they could take any captured Seminole's cattle or horses and consider them as their own property. Then came the heart of Jesup's message: the soldiers could sell any black person they captured.

So now the soldiers too became slave catchers. Even two Indian tribes agreed to help the soldiers track the Seminoles down if they were paid $50 for each black person they caught. The Cherokee Indians refused. "The Seminoles are our brothers," they said.

There followed another summer of sickness, hunger, and despair for the Seminoles.

Unlike the United States Army, the Seminoles could not replace a lost warrior. Their warriors were becoming fewer and fewer. Most of their cattle had already been taken. They could not plant crops in swamps. Osceola knew they were facing starvation. He himself was ill. How much longer could he lead his people?

8 The White Flag Dishonored

ONE DAY General Jesup received from Osceola the white plume of an egret and a peace pipe made of beads. Jesup knew what these two gifts meant. The pipe meant Osceola's wish to meet and talk of peace. The white feather meant that the Seminoles promised safety to the whites who came to the meeting ground.

The general knew this was his last chance to end the Seminole War and to emerge from this war a hero. He was prepared to use any method — fair or foul — to carry out his goal.

Once more he laid his plans.

He commanded his assistant, General Hernandez, to meet with Osceola twenty miles south of St. Augustine. He gave Hernandez a list of questions to be put to Osceola. If Osceola's replies were not satisfactory, Hernandez knew what he was to do.

The eventful day was October 21, 1837.

Osceola and the other Seminole chiefs put on their full ceremonial dress and shining silver jewelry. In their turbans they placed plumes of the egret to show they were meeting in peace. The white flag of truce that was flying in the gentle Florida breeze told Osceola that the white man was also meeting in peace. Like the plume of the egret, the flag of truce was a bond that no honorable man would betray.

Osceola and Hernandez greeted one another with friendly gestures. The Seminoles were asked to disarm. Osceola told his people to stack their weapons and they did.

This was to be a meeting to talk peace. But the first question Hernandez asked was:

"Are you prepared to deliver up the Negroes taken from the citizens?"

Osceola was stunned. He turned to the chief at his side and in a shaking voice said: "I am choked. You must speak for me . . ."

But there was no time for anyone to speak. Hernandez gave a signal. His troops, hidden nearby, moved in. Osceola was captured, together with twelve chiefs, seventy-five warriors, and six women.

One of the soldiers later wrote to a friend: "I shall never forget that day, nor the faces of Chief Osceola and the other Indians. We were outraged by the cowardly way he was betrayed into capture."

But General Jesup sat down and wrote to the Secretary of War. "I have the satisfaction to inform you that Osceola is my prisoner."

It was not a satisfaction that was shared by the American people. Newspapers across the nation reported in outrage the shameful capture of Osceola. "Dishonorable." "A violation of all that is noble in war." "We cannot forget that he was provoked by treachery and captured by treachery."

9 No Word for Good-bye

IN THE DAMP PRISON, Osceola was slowly dying. Yet so important a prisoner was he that when one of the Seminole chiefs escaped, Osceola was taken to a safer fortress. In December 1837, he was sent to Fort Moultrie near Charleston, South Carolina.

The story of Osceola spread across the land. More and more Americans were learning of his fight for his people and many became sympathetic toward his struggle.

Sometimes a guard would take Osceola out of his prison cell and let him sit by the water's edge. Sad and silent, Osceola watched the gulls swoop low, saw the blue heron fly over the grasses. He sat there motionless and heard the wind whisper through the trees. The gull, the heron, the wind — all free, but not Osceola.

Many people came to South Carolina to see the famous prisoner. Among them was George Catlin of New York. He was one of the most famous painters in America and he had come to paint Osceola's portrait. Soon the two men were friends. Osceola dressed in his finest clothes for the portrait and while Catlin painted, Osceola talked.

"It was always my pride to fight with the big generals," Osceola told Catlin. "These things that I wear remind me of them. I wore this plume when I defeated General Gaines, these spurs when I drove back General Clinch, and these moccasins when I whipped General Call."

On January 30, Osceola knew that he was dying. He could no longer speak, but with his hands he called for the chiefs and officers of the fort. He would die as he had lived — in dignity.

With great difficulty, he pulled on his buckskin tunic, his leggings, and his moccasins. He put on his war belt and carefully laid the war knife in its sheath by his side.

Then he called for red paint and a mirror. Slowly he painted one half of his face and throat, his wrists and the backs of his hand with the red paint of war. He smoothed the feathers in his turban and placed it upon his thick black hair.

Exhausted, he lay back upon his bed to rest for a moment. Then, with great effort, he smiled and held out his hand. The Seminoles and the whites came up to take his hand in silent farewell.

He lay still. Those standing near him thought him dead. But slowly his hand moved to his war belt and he drew out his knife. A deep silence filled the room as he laid the knife against his breast.

A moment later, he died.

There is no word for good-bye in the Seminole language.

At the age of thirty-four, Osceola was dead. But the war went on. For four more terrible years, the Seminoles led the fever-ridden troops an exhausting chase from swamp to swamp.

Finally, most of the Seminoles, hungry and homeless, agreed to be moved West — Seminole and black Seminole together.

But some three hundred Seminoles refused to come out of the swamps. They were not strong enough to continue to fight, but they never signed a peace treaty with the United States.

Above Osceola's grave in South Carolina, there is a marker placed there by the nation that fought him.

Osceola
Patriot and Warrior
Died at Ft. Moultrie
January 30, 1838

Today, deep in the Florida Everglades, wild animals still roam the woods. Many fish and alligators still swim the rivers. Snakes slither over the ground and birds fly overhead.

And there are still Seminoles there — the great, great grandchildren of the proud Seminole warriors who refused to surrender, who were never defeated.

Seminoles Awarded $12-Million For Florida Lands U. S. Seized

WASHINGTON, May 13 (AP) — The Seminole Indians, who owned most of Florida 150 years ago, were awarded $12,347,500 today for land taken from them by United States military forces.

The award, was made by the Indian Claims Commission on the basis of what the commission determined the land was worth a century and a half ago.

Sought Bigger Award

Unless it is appealed to the United States Court of Claims, the decision will end one of the longest and bitterest Indian disputes in the nation's history. The suit was filed 20 years ago.

The award was considerably less than the Indians had hoped for. The Seminoles contended in hearings last June that the 29.7 million acres taken from them, covering most of Florida, worth $47.9-million. Government appraisers set the value at $5.5-million.

The Seminoles' troubles began in 1816 when Gen. Andrew Jackson invaded Florida with Federal troops to punish the Indians for hiding fugitive slaves. Troubles continued after the United States bought Florida from Spain. The Indians contend Spain never owned the state and that the United States could not legally buy it.

The Indians went on the warpath to protect their rights and later, they contended, were tricked into two separate treaties in 1823 and 1832.

While many resettled in Oklahoma, others escaped into the cypress swamps of the Florida Everglades, where they have lived ever since.

The New York Times, Thursday, May 14, 1970.

Tecumseh

1 The Young Tecumseh

IN OLD PIQUA, a village of wigwams and bark cabins near the Mad River of Ohio, Tecumseh was born. From the time of his birth in March 1768, to the time of his death forty-five years later, there would be little peace for Tecumseh and his people, the Shawnee Nation.

While Tecumseh was still a very young child his father taught him many skills. Before he was six he had learned how to make a bow for his arrows, how to throw the tomahawk, how to fish and hunt.

Tecumseh's father was not always home to teach him. For his father was a Shawnee war chief and was often away fighting the white settlers who came into the Shawnee land south of the Ohio River.

Tecumseh.
A portrait based on descriptions of the Shawnee chief.

By the time Tecumseh was six years old, war had broken out between these settlers and the Shawnees. The fighting was fierce and both sides lost many men. In the end the Shawnee commander, Cornstalk, was forced to sign a treaty of peace. In this treaty the Shawnees had to give up all their land south of the Ohio River.

Settlers from Virginia swarmed into this land that had been taken from the Shawnees. So the Shawnees retreated to the land north of the Ohio River. This would now be their home. The treaty promised that no settlers would come into this northern land.

It was a promise quickly broken. The settlers pressed on, wanting still more land to build farms and towns. In spite of the treaty, they seized Shawnee land north of the Ohio River.

When Tecumseh was six, he saw his father die. He saw his father shot down by a white man for refusing to be his hunting guide.

He would always remember his mother's voice: "Avenge the death of your father! Become a whirlwind and a storm! Scatter desolation and death among the whites!"

The murder of her husband made Tecumseh's mother sad and sick. A few months later, her eighth child — the boy, Laulewasika, was born. She left the care of her baby and her other children to Tecumseh's older sister. A few years later, still overwhelmed with grief, she left the village forever.

A Shawnee chief. Shawnee women used porcupine
quills to make the designs which decorate his clothing.

It was not long before Tecumseh lost another important person in his life.

Above all other men, Tecumseh had always admired Cornstalk, war leader of the Shawnees. Cornstalk had been at peace with the whites since the signing of the treaty. Then Tecumseh heard that Cornstalk had been killed while visiting an American fort. A mob of soldiers, angered by the killing of a white man, had shot the Shawnee leader.

Near Old Piqua was the village of Old Chillicothe, ruled by Chief Blackfish. It was fortunate for Tecumseh that now Blackfish adopted the lonely boy and treated him as his own son. Tecumseh divided his time between the two villages.

His sister taught him to be honest, to respect the rights of others, and to obey his elders.

Blackfish taught him valuable skills of warfare.

In both Piqua and Old Chillicothe the old people took Tecumseh into their cabins and wigwams and taught him how to speak his thoughts clearly and with force.

The older Shawnees were grateful for Tecumseh's kindness to them. When the cold winds of winter began to blow, the young boy went from one village to the other, patching the old people's wigwams and cabins, bringing them meat to eat and deerskins to make warm clothing and moccasins.

But this small time of peace did not last.

Tecumseh was a boy of eight when, in 1776, the Americans began their War of Independence against the British. The British promised not to take Indian land, so many Indian nations fought with the British. The Shawnees too fought the Americans.

In 1780, the war came to Old Piqua. Tecumseh watched his village vanish in flames, as American soldiers drove the Shawnees from their homes.

In 1781, Tecumseh took part in his first battle.

Here, Tecumseh saw his older brother wounded. Frightened, he fled from the battlefield. That night he called himself a coward and vowed he would never again show fear. From that day on, Tecumseh would be the last to leave the field of battle.

With the end of the Revolutionary War came a new stream of settlers moving west onto Indian land. They came in greater and greater numbers, taking more and more Indian land in the north. The Shawnees fought to hold on to their hunting lands, to keep the settlers out. Tecumseh, only fifteen, joined the band of Shawnees who attacked the flatboats carrying the settlers down the Ohio.

After one such attack on a settlers' boat, the Shawnees burned a captive at the stake. Tecumseh watched with horror. He hated the white men with all his being. What had white men brought to his people but suffering? But he also knew compassion, and senseless torture sickened him.

Suddenly, without a thought to his age or to his lesser place in the tribe, he was on his feet, crying to the older men that what they had done was not an act of courage nor an act of men. "An animal shows such cruelty to the helpless," he cried, "A man does not!"

The older men were shamed by the words of the fifteen-year-old boy.

Tecumseh began to learn the power of his own thoughts spoken in his own words. This would be a powerful weapon to sway men and change the course of history.

2 A Leader Grows

INTO the Northwest Territory, into Indian Land, came the settlers. By boat and wagon, in carts and on foot they came — ten thousand a year. And as the wave of settlers grew, so grew Tecumseh's leadership in the Shawnee struggle to hold onto their land.

By the time Tecumseh was twenty-three, he had taken part in many battles against the frontiersmen.

The settlers turned to General Arthur St. Clair for help against the Indians. In 1791, General St. Clair led an army of more than eight thousand men to the Wabash River. Tecumseh was one of the first three warriors to break through the American lines in the battle that destroyed St. Clair's powerful army. This was so great a defeat for the Americans that for a long while, settlers were discouraged from coming to the Northwest Territory.

The following year, Tecumseh's older brother Chief Chees traveled south to help the Cherokee Indians fight the settlers in Tennessee. He sent word for Tecumseh to join him. When Chief Chees

was killed, Tecumseh replaced him as leader of all the Shawnee warriors in the South. Tecumseh led them in battle in Tennessee, in Mississippi, Alabama, Georgia, and Florida.

Two years later, still another brother was killed at Fallen Timbers. There the mighty army of General "Mad" Anthony Wayne defeated the hopelessly outnumbered Indians. Not satisfied with victory, General Wayne burned Indian villages, one after the other. After the Battle of Fallen Timbers, Wayne called the defeated Indians to a council at Greenville, Ohio.

To this council came a thousand Indians from twelve different tribes. They signed a treaty in which they had to give up two-thirds of Ohio. In exchange for their land, the Indians received $20,000 in goods and the promise of an additional $10,000.

Tecumseh had refused to go to the council at Greenville. He refused to take part in the giving up of this Indian land. He would not accept what the other chiefs had done. They had no right to sell the land of their fathers.

Tecumseh spoke against the treaty at every opportunity. Though he was only 27, he spoke with the wisdom and power of a great chief, and more and more Indians listened.

Members of the United Society of Believers. They are called Shakers because when they worship, they tremble and chant a wordless song. The Shawnee Prophet was greatly influenced by Shaker missionaries.

A few years later while visiting his sister in Ohio, Tecumseh came to know the settler James Galloway and his family. Galloway had brought three hundred books to his wilderness home. Tecumseh was curious about them and interested to know what they contained.

It was Galloway's daughter, Rebecca, who became his teacher. In time, Tecumseh learned to speak and read English with ease. Eagerly, he read Galloway's books. For Tecumseh was thirsty for any knowledge that would help him better understand and deal with the white man.

After a time, Rebecca came to think of Tecumseh as the most remarkable man she had ever met. And Tecumseh began to think of her as a woman he wanted to marry.

Following the Shawnee custom, Tecumseh asked James Galloway for permission to marry his daughter. Galloway liked Tecumseh. He thought him the most intelligent man he had ever met. He advised Tecumseh to ask Rebecca himself.

Rebecca agreed to marry Tecumseh — but only on one condition. He must give up his life as an Indian. He must be willing to live as a white man.

Tecumseh needed time to think. He searched his mind and his heart. Then he made his decision.

He returned to Rebecca and told her he could not leave his people. He was an Indian. He did not want to live as a white man.

3 "Make the Sun Stand Still"

Tecumseh's people were pushed farther and farther West as the white man came from the East. Farmers, workers, old soldiers, outlaws, and adventurers came, paying two dollars an acre for farm land where the Indians had lived. They laid out towns where the Indians hunted.

With the white men came their whiskey. Tecumseh saw what whiskey did to his people. He saw how it destroyed their bodies and how it turned brother against brother.

Tecumseh heard terrible stories about his youngest brother Laulewasika, whom he had not seen since childhood. He learned that Laulewasika had become a drunkard.

Then, in 1805, Tecumseh heard something even

more strange about his brother. Laulewasika had given up whiskey and turned to religion. He now called himself the Prophet and claimed a hundred followers.

Tecumseh had to see this for himself. He went to his brother's village. There he heard Laulewasika tell his people to stop warring among themselves and to stop drinking the white man's whiskey.

Tecumseh saw the faces of the Prophet's followers. He saw that they believed every word his brother said.

For some time now, Tecumseh had a dream — a hope that if all the Indian Nations from many tribes could come together to form *one* confederation, they would be better able to protect their land against the oncoming white settlers.

Tecumseh saw how the Prophet could help with his plan. He and his brother joined forces. They would unite all the nations in the land. Then they could keep the white men from taking another inch of their country!

The two brothers moved to Greenville, Ohio, where the chiefs had signed the hated treaty.

In 1800, the western-most part of the Northwest Territory became known as Indiana Territory. William Henry Harrison, who would later be President of the United States, was made Governor of this newly formed territory. Governor Harrison became worried as more and more of the Prophet's followers

The Shawnee Prophet, Laulewasika, commanding the sun to stand still.

came to Greenville. Too many Indians in one place might mean trouble. Perhaps if he could weaken the Prophet's power, he could disperse the Indians.

He had a plan. In April 1806, Governor Harrison sent a message to the Delaware Indians: "If he is really a prophet," he said, "ask him to cause the sun to stand still, the moon to alter its course, the rivers to cease to flow or the dead to rise from their graves. If he does these things, you may then believe he has been sent from God."

Harrison's challenge excited the Prophet. He would use the challenge to help unite the nations. The Prophet found out that there was soon to be a total eclipse of the sun. He even knew the day on which the scientists expected the eclipse — June 16.

He sent word to the nations that the Prophet would cause the sun to darken and that they could witness this miracle themselves.

On June 16, a great crowd came to Greenville. The Prophet appeared, dressed in dark flowing robes.

He pointed to the sun. At 11:32, the moon began to move slowly across the face of the sun. In the growing darkness, the people looked at each other wordlessly and gazed at the Prophet in awe. Then the Prophet cried out, "Master of Life! Take your hand from the face of the sun and cause it to glow once more!"

When the light returned and the sun shone brightly, the crowds stole silently away, too full of wonder to speak.

News of the Prophet's power spread like a wind across the land. More and more Indians joined him in Greenville.

Tecumseh's chance had come at last. Together with the Prophet, he would unite all tribes into a single force with a single purpose — to defend *Indian* land.

4 The Warrior
and the Governor

N ow was the time, Tecumseh believed, to go among the Indians of the East, West, South, and North, and to urge them to unite.

But first, Tecumseh thought, the Prophet's village at Greenville had to be moved elsewhere. Greenville was too close to white settlements and every move made by the Indians was watched and reported to Governor Harrison.

So a new village, called Prophet's Town, was built. It was set up where the Wabash and the Tippecanoe Rivers joined, closer to Harrison but farther from his informers.

In the spring of 1808, Tecumseh and his brother traveled across the central plains, stopping now with one group, moving on to another. At every council fire, Tecumseh spoke and his words stirred those who listened:

One by one the tribes are being crushed by the wagon wheels of settlers who come to take our land from us. We must be ready to face them with a great army. There must be one mighty force made up of all the tribes. Only in that way can we save the land of our fathers.

To the nations along the Illinois River, to the nations of Wisconsin, Tecumseh spoke again and again of his plan for an Indian confederation so strong and so united that it could defend its land.

In many villages those who listened welcomed this idea. Some chiefs, however, wanted nothing to do with war. Others feared they would lose the leadership of their tribe.

Tecumseh traveled thousands of miles — to Florida to speak to the Seminoles, to Missouri where the Osage tribes gathered to listen to him, and finally to New York and the Iroquois.

He felt he had made progress in the year of his travels. Though his ideas were not accepted everywhere, he had sowed the seeds for the greatest Indian confederation in the history of his people.

Now, as he turned toward Indiana and Prophet's Town, he knew there was still much work to be done. To those who had turned down his ideas, he would appeal again. To those who had agreed to follow him, he would come again to make sure they would not weaken.

On the way back to Indiana, Tecumseh received shocking news. While he had been away, in the summer of 1809, Governor Harrison had met with several chiefs at Fort Wayne. He had supplied them with whiskey and pressured them to sign a new treaty.

For a little more than $10,000, the Indians had sold three million acres of Indian land. Much of it owned by nations whose chiefs were not even at Fort Wayne! With the lost land went some of the Shawnees' best hunting grounds.

"That land belonged to all the Indians," Tecumseh said. "No one chief has the right to sell a piece of it!" Tecumseh sent word to nations near and far that he refused to honor the treaty of Fort Wayne. By the spring of 1810, a thousand warriors had flocked to Prophet's Town, ready to fight if the Americans tried to settle on the land.

Tecumseh decided on a bold action. He would go to Vincennes and confront the governor.

On August 11, 1810, Tecumseh, the Prophet, and three hundred armed warriors arrived in eighty canoes at Vincennes. The warriors had painted their faces, red, the color of war.

The meeting was to take place at a grove near the governor's headquarters. Tecumseh picked thirty of his warriors to accompany him and his brother. Many important officials were already there.

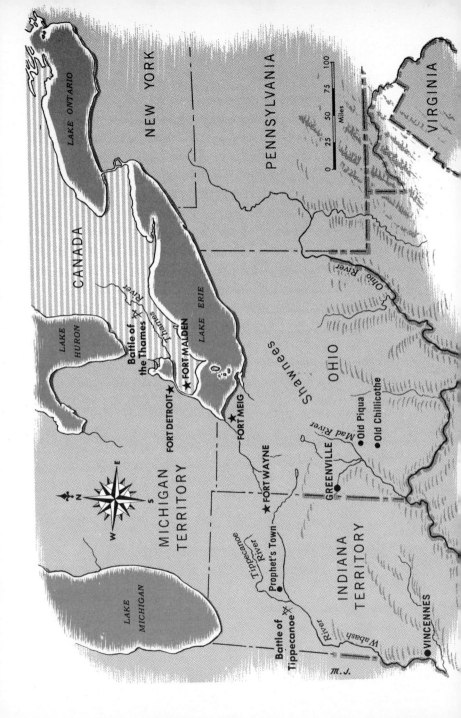

Tecumseh was first to speak. He directed his words to Governor Harrison. He went over the history of every treaty ever made with the Indians and told how unfair each treaty proved to be. He spoke of what took place after the treaties were signed — how Indians who were supposed to be protected by the treaties were killed, how their land was taken away, how the Indians were given spoiled food, how death had come to many after they were exposed to smallpox, a disease unknown to the Indians before the white man came.

He spoke of his plan to unite the Indians:

The being within me tells me that once there were no white men on all this land. The land was never divided but belonged to all, for the use of everyone. No tribe has a right to sell, even to each other, much less to strangers who demand all and will not do with less. Sell a country? Why not sell the air, the clouds, and the great sea as well as the earth? Did not the Great Spirit make them all for the use of his children?

Your United States has set an example for us. Your country has formed a union out of seventeen states. You have done what we hope to do, yet you tell us we should not.

Then Harrison began to speak. He claimed that the United States had always been fair in dealing with the Indians.

At these words, Tecumseh leaped to his feet. "It is false," he cried. "He lies!"

The moment was tense. The governor drew his sword from its sheath and stepped forward. Tecumseh's thirty warriors drew their tomahawks from their belts and awaited their leader's signal.

Harrison declared that the council was over. Without another word, he walked toward his headquarters.

Tecumseh led his warriors back to their camp. The next morning he sent apologies for his outburst to Governor Harrison.

The governor accepted the apology and came to visit Tecumseh. Tecumseh invited him to sit on a bench beside him. As they talked, Tecumseh moved closer to Harrison. The governor was forced to move farther down the bench. Again, Tecumseh moved closer. Again, Harrison moved away. This went on until the governor was at the end of the bench. When he was at this point, he objected. Tecumseh said grimly, "Now you know how we feel. This is exactly what you are doing to us — pushing the Indians off their own land!"

5 "Let Us Unite"

THE END of the Revolutionary War had not brought lasting peace to Great Britain and America. It looked as if they would soon be at war again.

Tecumseh felt the British could help his people fight the American soldiers. He went to Fort Malden, the British outpost in Canada. There he talked to Major Taylor about his Indian confederation. He asked for arms and supplies in case America and Britain went to war. He felt that the meeting was a success. Back home he told his people that the British had promised to help them.

It was time, Tecumseh felt, to journey to the South once more to meet with the Indian nation. And on August 5, 1811, he set off down the Wabash River with twenty-four warriors.

His journey took him down the Ohio and Mississippi Rivers, through Tennessee to Mississippi, Alabama, Georgia, Florida, back north to the Carolinas, to the Ozark Mountains of Arkansas and Missouri, north into Iowa, and then home. He traveled by pony, in canoe, and on foot.

Sometimes as many as 5,000 Indians gathered to listen to him. He spoke to the Choctaws and the Chickasaws, urging them to live in peace with all the other Indians. He told how the Americans were grabbing up land. He asked that the tribes fight on the side of the British should there be war between the United States and Great Britain.

His words were forceful:

Where today are the once powerful tribes of our people? They have vanished before the greed of the white man, as snow before a summer sun. Look over their once beautiful country and what do you see? Nothing but the ruins of the paleface destroyers! So it will be with you, Choctaw and Chickasaw! Soon your mighty forests will be cut down to fence in the land which the white intruders dare to call their own!

And to the Creeks, he cried:

You were once a mighty people. Now your tomahawks have no edge, your bows and arrows are buried with your fathers. Brush from your eyes the sleep of slavery! Once more strike for vengeance — once more for your country!

His speech was moving. Half the warriors were ready to join him. But the chief of the Upper Creeks did not agree with Tecumseh. He would not approve Tecumseh's confederation.

"Your blood is white," Tecumseh cried in anger. "You have taken my talk but you do not mean to fight. I know the reason. You do not believe the Great Spirit has sent me. You shall know! When I return to my village on the Tippecanoe I shall stamp my foot and the very earth will tremble."

On the night of December 16, 1811, a rumbling was heard and the Mississippi Valley shook from an earthquake. The Creeks whispered in awe and the word was passed from one tribe to another: "Tecumseh has reached the Tippecanoe."

But Tecumseh was still on the move. He traveled south to the village of the Seminoles who swore to join him. But he had no such luck with the Cherokee or the Osage or the Iowa Indians.

He headed for home, footsore and heartsick, still unable to unite all his people. He had traveled thousands of miles in six months. Mountains and swamps had not stopped him. Rain and snow had not slowed him.

Wearily he reached Prophet's Town on a cold, gray day in February 1812.

He could not believe his eyes. Prophet's Town was in ruins — the fields burned, the wigwams and council house destroyed.

That night Tecumseh found out what had happened. Harrison had waited until Tecumseh left on his journey south. Then he marched his army to Prophet's Town.

The Indians feared Harrison's attack and knew they were hopelessly outnumbered. Tecumseh had clearly instructed the Prophet not to allow any fighting. There was disagreement among the warriors, however. Some felt their only hope was to launch a surprise attack of their own. And they did.

The Indians had only 450 men; the Americans more than a thousand. The battle — called the Battle of Tippecanoe — which lasted only a day was a victory for Harrison and his army. But before he returned to Vincennes, Harrison destroyed Prophet's Town.

Not satisfied with smashing the houses, Harrison's army destroyed all the corn the Indians had harvested. Tippecanoe was not a big battle, but Harrison turned it into a great victory for himself. He wrote to the Secretary of War: "The Indians had never sustained so severe a defeat since their acquaintance with the white people." Later when Harrison ran for President of the United States, John Tyler was his candidate for Vice President. Their campaign slogan was: "Tippecanoe and Tyler too." It helped them to be elected.

The defeat at Tippecanoe was a terrible blow to Tecumseh. He had lost his headquarters, his supplies, almost everything. It was the kind of small warfare he had hoped to avoid. He wanted to fight

The Battle of Tippecanoe in which Tecumseh's forces were defeated.

the soldiers when he could have a strong, united Indian confederation.

He gathered his people around him where the mission house once stood. And he made this vow:

"I stand upon the ashes of my home. I summon the spirits of the braves who have fallen as they protected their homes. I swear once more the hatred of an avenger."

Tecumseh held the Prophet responsible for the tragedy.

Tecumseh had told him again and again that there was to be no fighting until he returned. The Prophet had not followed orders to prevent the battle. Tecumseh sent him away.

The Prophet wandered west, his followers and his influence gone.

"Tippecanoe and Tyler too," the campaign slogan used by William Henry Harrison when he ran for the office of President. Harrison's campaign was noted for torchlight parades, hard cider, and barbecues.

6 In the Army of the King

THE WAR OF 1812 between America and Great Britain was declared on June 18. Most Indians sided with the British for reasons Tecumseh put eloquently:

Here is a chance that will never occur again, a chance for the Indians of North America to form ourselves into one great combination and cast our lot with the British in this war. And should they conquer and again get mastery of all North America, our rights to at least a portion of the land of our fathers would be respected by the British King. If they should not win and the whole country should pass into the hands of the Long Knives, it will not be many years before our last hunting ground will be taken from us and we will be driven toward the setting sun.

Thousands of warriors from many tribes came to join Tecumseh in the battles that followed.

General Isaac Brock, the lieutenant-governor of Canada, took command of Fort Malden on August 13. His first action was to call a meeting of his top officers. When Brock and Tecumseh were introduced, they shook hands in friendship. Tecumseh felt that he could place his confidence in the tall, rugged general, and Brock saw immediately the qualities that made Tecumseh a great leader.

Brock asked the officers what they thought the British should do next. "Attack Fort Detroit," Tecumseh said. He knew that the American general, William Hull, had three thousand soldiers at Fort Detroit. He also knew that General Hull was not a fighter and that he would be terrified by a sudden attack. With the point of his knife, Tecumseh drew a map of Fort Detroit on a piece of elm bark and described its defenses.

Brock listened to the arguments of the other men. Only one of the officers agreed with Tecumseh that Detroit could be captured.

Brock made up his mind quickly. He would follow Tecumseh's plan. The British and the Indians would move against Detroit.

Under a great oak tree on a broad meadow just outside Fort Malden, General Brock faced Tecumseh's warriors.

"Welcome to the army of the Great King," he began. Then he told them that the Americans wanted

Fort Dearborn, built to protect the land taken from the Indians by the Treaty of Greenville.

to drive not only the Indians but the British from the land. He told them he meant to carry the war across the river. He would help recover Indian land.

Then Tecumseh spoke. "The Americans are our enemies," he said. "They came to us hungry and they cut off the hands of our brothers who gave them corn. We gave them rivers of fish, and they poisoned our fountains. We gave them forest-clad mountains and valleys full of game, and in return what did they give our warriors and our women? Whiskey and trinkets and a grave!"

That afternoon, the 14th of August, Brock and Tecumseh led their armies north.

Tecumseh and his warriors crossed the river. They surrounded Detroit, cutting off all approaches by land.

Brock took Tecumseh aside and told him of a trick he had played. He had let a British messenger be captured by the Americans on purpose. The British messenger told General Hull that a war party of five thousand Indians was coming to fight against him.

Tecumseh smiled. He would add further trickery to Brock's plan. He assembled his entire force of six hundred Indians and told them what to do. Immediately the woods were filled with terrifying war whoops. Three times, the Indians ran back and forth, four and five abreast, in full view of the American fort. The running Indians, seen first in one place, then in another, convinced General Hull that there were at least five thousand Indians ready to charge from the forest.

Hull ordered the white flag of surrender raised over Fort Detroit.

Brock and Tecumseh were stunned. They had expected a fierce fight and had not been at all sure of defeating an army twice the size of their own. It was a great victory for Brock and Tecumseh.

The British general understood the part the Shawnee chief had played in the victory. As their soldiers and warriors watched, Brock gave Tecumseh his own silk sash and his pair of beautiful pistols. Tecumseh presented Brock with a beaded belt, which the general kept the rest of his life.

7 "I Am Tecumseh"

GENERAL BROCK moved his headquarters to a house in Detroit, and Tecumseh was given a parlor and a bedroom on the second floor.

The days that followed were among the few peaceful times Tecumseh knew in his life. He laughed a lot, smoked his pipe, and enjoyed pleasant meals with the officers.

In his report, Brock wrote of Tecumseh: "A more gallant warrior does not exist. He has the admiration of everyone who talks with him."

But the peaceful days were soon to end. Brock left for the Niagara border to stop an American invasion there. He left Colonel Procter in charge of Detroit.

Procter and Brock were as different as night and day. Procter was a vain, slow-thinking man who thought a great deal of himself and very little of Indians.

Tecumseh knew he would have trouble with Procter. And twenty-four hours after Brock had left Detroit, trouble arose.

Colonel Procter ordered that every American in the captured city of Detroit would have to swear loyalty to the British Crown. One of the leading American citizens in Detroit was Father Gabriel, a priest and a friend to the Indians. He refused. "I have taken one oath to support the Constitution of the United States," he said, "and I cannot take another. Do with me as you please."

Procter threw him into prison.

Tecumseh demanded that Procter release the prisoner. If Procter did not, Tecumseh would take all his warriors back to the Wabash River. "General Brock would understand my reasons," Tecumseh said.

Procter quickly ordered Father Gabriel set free.

But even though he had won this small victory, Tecumseh knew that he had only increased the bad feelings between himself and the colonel.

In September 1812, Tecumseh began another journey south. He thought that if the Creek Indians could wage war in the South, the American Long Knives would have two wars on their hands and chance of success would be greater.

Once more the Creeks listened to his words:

Why doubt our power to defeat the Americans? We have done it in the North. Our villages will again be safe. Our hunting grounds will be as free as the arrow in the air, as the flight of the eagle in the sky. The British are our brothers. They do not wish to make us live in the houses of the palefaces to hew their wood or draw their water. They will not change our customs or drive us from our homes.

The Creeks were now ready to fight.

When Tecumseh returned to Fort Malden in April of 1813, he led three thousand warriors. Never before had the Indians brought together such an army. All they needed was an able British commander.

The news Tecumseh received on his return made his heart heavy with sorrow. His friend, General Brock, had been killed in battle. And the man he

Two Shawnee girls sketched by a German artist when he passed through Shawnee territory on his way West.

despised, Colonel Procter, was now in command, promoted to general.

The British and Indians were soon to face Tecumseh's old enemy, General Harrison. How could a man like Procter lead them to victory?

The battle took place at Fort Meigs. Once more Tecumseh resorted to trickery. Though his warriors numbered fifteen hundred, he sent this message to General Harrison: "I have with me eight hundred braves. You have an equal number in your hiding place. Come out with them and give me battle. You talked like a brave when we met at Vincennes, but now you hide behind logs, and in the earth, like a ground hog. Give me your answer."

No answer came from the fort. Nevertheless Tecumseh led an attack on the Long Knives and he was successful. But when he returned to the fort, he came upon a scene that filled him with rage. A group of Indians was torturing thirty-six American soldiers.

Tecumseh charged at them at a gallop. He grabbed a knife from one warrior and sent others sprawling to the ground. Standing between the Indians and their prisoners, he shouted, "Are there no men here?"

Tecumseh was heartsick. He blamed Procter for doing nothing to stop the torture.

Tecumseh stormed into the general's tent. He demanded to know why the general had not prevented the torturing of the Americans.

"Your Indians cannot be controlled," Procter

said, in his haughtiest tone. "They cannot be commanded."

"You lie!" Tecumseh cried. "You call yourself a *general*? You are nothing but a squaw!"

It was the worst insult an Indian could speak.

"Begone!" Tecumseh said. "You are unfit to command. Go and put on petticoats. I conquer to save, and you to murder!"

Later Procter tried to get back at Tecumseh by issuing orders that the Indians be given horsemeat to eat instead of beef.

When Tecumseh heard about this, he went to see Procter. He didn't bother to tell Procter that it was Tecumseh and his warriors who were carrying the heavy load of this war. He simply touched Procter's sword, then touched his own tomahawk, and said, "You are Procter. I am Tecumseh."

Procter understood that Tecumseh meant to fight him, hand to hand. Immediately he gave orders that the food given to the Indians and the British was to be the same.

Now Procter was afraid that the Indians would desert him. He heard that the British had lost a battle on Lake Erie. It was the most important battle of the war. But he did not dare tell Tecumseh the truth about the battle. And at the same time, Procter secretly began making plans to retreat.

But Tecumseh knew Procter's plans. He assembled his warriors on the Fort Malden parade ground, and, looking straight at Procter, he said, "You always

Tecumseh saving white men from being tortured.

told us to remain here and take care of our lands. It made our hearts glad to hear you say that was your wish. You always told us that you would never draw your foot off British ground. But now we see that you are pulling back, that you are getting ready to fall back before you even have sight of the enemy. We must compare your conduct to a fat dog that carries its tail on its back, but when frightened, drops it between its legs and runs."

Tecumseh saw Procter's face turn pale.

"Listen!" he continued. "We wish to remain here and fight the enemy. You have the arms and ammunition which our great father sent for his red children. If you have an idea of going away, give them to us, and you may go, and welcome. The Great Spirit gave to our ancestors the lands which we possess. We are determined to defend them, and if it is His will, our bones shall whiten on them, but we will never give up."

Badly frightened, Procter made for his quarters. Now he feared the Indians almost as much as he feared the Americans.

Tecumseh was not alone in wanting to defend the fort. The British soldiers wanted to fight for their fort — not retreat.

Procter felt his soldiers' anger rise toward him. He knew Tecumseh hated him. Procter said he would not retreat altogether; he would make a stand near the Thames River.

One night, while Tecumseh was dining with the

officers, a messenger came in with the news that a huge American fleet was sailing up the Detroit River.

Tecumseh rose, put his hands on the pistols General Brock had given him and said to Procter, "We must go to meet the enemy and prevent them from coming here. We must not retreat. If you take us from this place you will lead us to the mercy of the Long Knives. I am tired of it all. Every word you say blows to nothing, like the smoke from our pipes. You are like the crawfish that does not know how to walk straight ahead!"

Procter assembled his men and at once began his move to the Thames River.

Tecumseh assembled his army of a thousand warriors and followed the British.

On October 4, Tecumseh learned that Harrison was approaching the Thames River with a large force.

The night was chilly. Tecumseh sat with his warriors around the fire. Suddenly he looked up and said, "Brother warriors, we are about to enter an engagement from which I shall not return. My body will remain on the field of battle."

Both sides spent the next morning planning the battle which was to come.

Tecumseh told his own warriors to "be brave, stand firm, and shoot straight."

In anticipation of a good fight, Tecumseh's spirits rose. Then he walked up to General Procter and said in a friendly voice, "Have a big heart. Tell your young men to be firm and all will be well."

At four o'clock in the afternoon, the British and the Indians heard the clear notes of the American bugles sounding through the woods.

Then the Americans charged.

Procter jumped into his carriage and fled. But most of his soldiers and all of the Indians remained to fight. And while the gunfire burst all around them in the woods, Tecumseh's voice could be heard, urging his men forward to attack.

He was wounded again and again, and still he battled on.

But before the battle was over, Tecumseh was dead.

In the years that followed, the Indian nations grew smaller and smaller. Soon towns stood where hunting grounds had been.

But it would take more than death to erase the memory of Tecumseh. The Indiana *Sentinel* of December 2, 1880 said:

Tecumseh was a great man. He was truly great — and his greatness was his own, unassisted by science or the aids of education. As a statesman, a warrior, and a patriot, we shall not look upon his like again.

Cochise

1 Days of Peace

COCHISE was at peace.

The most powerful Apache chief was at peace with the white man. His warriors had not fought the white men in five years.

Now, in 1860, signs of peace were everywhere in Cochise's village. The *wickiups,* the round houses covered with thatch and deerskin, were sturdy and well built. If this were war time, the wickiups would be made in a much simpler, cruder way so that the tribe could break up camp and be gone in a matter of minutes.

There were many Apache tribes in the land that is now Arizona. Cochise's tribe was called the Chiricahua Apaches and though they were the smallest tribe they were the most powerful of them all.

At this time Cochise was nearly fifty years old, yet he had the strength and the look of a far younger man. He stood over six-feet tall — taller than any of

Cochise.
A portrait based on descriptions of the Apache chief.

his warriors. He had the straight powerful body of a fighting man and the deep intelligent eyes of a thinking man.

He was born in 1814. Early in life, he began to train for the hunt and the battle.

He learned how to make weapons, how to use them with speed and accuracy, and how to dodge them just as skillfully.

He learned to be like a rock — silent and still for hours; to make no sound when wounded, no sound as he attacked.

He learned to be like a deer — to run for miles, for hours over hot, sandy desert and rough mountain places without stopping for rest, food, or drink.

Heat, cold, hunger, thirst — all these he knew how to live with. But even then, he was not a warrior.

Like every young boy of his tribe, he had to show he could live alone. For two weeks, alone in the deserts and mountains, he ate and drank only what he could find in the barren land.

Yet even then he was not a warrior. Four times he had to go to battle — not to fight, but to run errands for the fighting warriors.

After that, and only then, could an Apache boy call himself a warrior.

Now, as Cochise watched the children of his tribe playing their games of war, he was glad that soon new warriors would add strength to his small tribe.

"Not that five or six warriors — or even fifty or sixty! — would make much difference," Cochise

94

An Apache woman building the frame of a wickiup. On the left is a completed wickiup, with a covering over the basic material called thatch.

thought, "compared to the number of white men who have come to our land.

"How can I even number them?" he thought. It would be like trying to count drops of rain or grains of desert sand. There seemed to be no end to the white man.

No wonder it seemed this way to Cochise. For hundreds of years the Apache tribes had roamed these deserts, these mountains, these canyons and forests. Then came the Mexicans. The Apaches were constantly at war with them, but in the end they were able to keep the Mexicans off Apache land.

But then, from the East came the Americans. These deserts, these mountains, these canyons and forests, they said, were now theirs.

Cochise and his people did not know that the United States, only 72 years old in 1848, was involved in a grim war with Mexico. The Apaches did not know that after the war, and after the purchase of land from Mexico, there was a new boundary between the United States and Mexico. Nearly all the

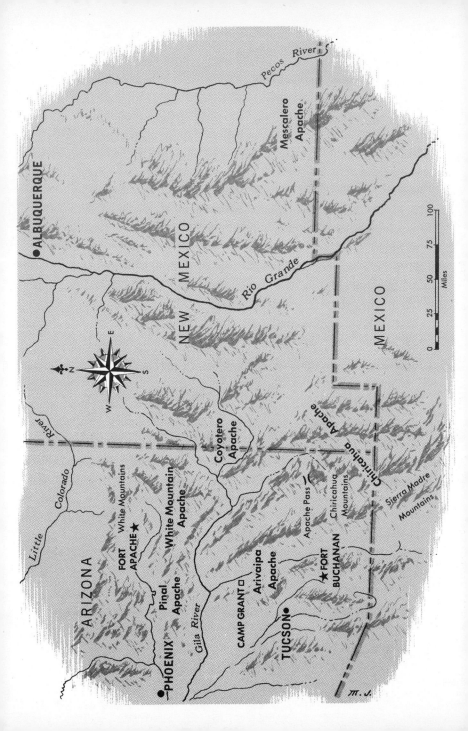

Apache land was on the United States side of the boundary, in what is now Arizona and New Mexico.

In that land lived fifty thousand Indians of various tribes, among them, the Apache tribes. Until 1853, there had been only five thousand white men.

Now the white men poured into Apache country.

Settlers came. They built cattle ranches and grazed their cattle on Apache land.

Miners came. They dug into Indian land for gold and silver. Then when the Apaches tried to protect their land, soldiers came. The soldiers built forts to protect the ranchers and miners.

Ranchers, miners, soldiers — all invaders on Apache land.

At first the Apaches had tried to fight the Americans as they had the Mexicans. But the Americans had deadly weapons and it seemed there was no end to the number of men who fired them.

In the two years, it was alarming how many Apaches were killed.

As his people mourned the fallen warriors, Cochise would spend long hours thinking sadly that his tribe might soon become only a name lost to memory.

"We cannot fight them or destroy them," he thought. "They grow stronger while we grow weaker."

Cochise came to a very important decision. He would make peace with the white man. Only in that way could his tribe survive.

Of all the many Apache tribes, not one was at peace with the white men. To think of peace was unheard of. Could Cochise possibly convince the white men that his offer of peace was sincere?

At Fort Buchanan, not far from what is now the city of Tucson, Cochise met with an American colonel. Colonel Steen was the officer in charge of the fort. He was an intelligent man who understood how important peace with the Apaches could be. Steen trusted Cochise and peace was made.

And now, for five years, Cochise saw to it that peace was kept.

All around Cochise's tribe — across the mountains to the north, down the valley to the east, other Apache tribes kept up their war with the white men. They felt the only way to stop the whites from coming to the land was to fight them. The warring tribes scornfully called the peaceful Chiricahua Apaches "Grandmothers to Americans."

Not all of the Chiricahua warriors believed that peace was the way to survive. Some still yearned for war with the Americans.

But every warrior knew that Cochise had pledged to keep his peace and that he would never break that pledge. Truth and honor had a value among all Apaches, but in no man was it stronger than in Cochise. Even his enemies knew that Cochise never told a lie, never broke a promise, and showed no mercy to anyone who did.

2 Under the White Flag

O N A DAY in October of 1860, trouble came to Cochise's country. It began when a little boy named Micky Free was kidnaped. The kidnaping took place not far from the village where the Chiricahua Apaches lived.

Micky's mother was a Mexican woman who had been captured by a northern tribe called the Pinal Apaches. Micky's father was a Pinal Apache who died when Micky was still a baby. After the death of her husband, Micky's mother took her child and ran away from the Pinal Apaches.

She came to a ranch owned by John Ward, a white man, and began keeping house for him. Ward adopted her son, but the Pinal Apaches said that Micky was an Apache. They vowed to get him back.

John Ward was not at home on that fateful day the Pinal Apaches came to his ranch. One of them snatched up Micky and galloped off. The others drove off Ward's cattle and horses. The Pinal Apaches lived to the west of Ward's ranch. But cleverly, they rode first to the east, then turned west and headed home.

When Ward discovered the boy was missing, he swore revenge. He followed the tracks of the horses and cattle and saw that they led eastward — in the direction of the Chiricahua village. "Cochise!" Ward cried.

John Ward was stubborn and quick-tempered. It was said that once he made his mind up about anything, he never changed it. It was known too how he hated Indians.

He galloped to Fort Buchanan, twelve miles away. Unfortunately, Colonel Steen was no longer in command of the fort. Ward told the new commander, Colonel Morrison, what had happened.

"It was Cochise who stole my kid and my cattle," he said.

Morrison was surprised. Was Ward sure that Cochise had kidnaped the boy? Didn't Ward know that Cochise had kept peace faithfully?

It wasn't possible to reason with Ward. The idea that there could be peace and honor with the Indians was plain nonsense to him. To him, they were savages.

He demanded that Morrison act fast.

But three months passed before Morrison finally did anything.

A Butterfield stage coach. One of these specially built coaches was the first to carry mail through Apache country.

Who knows but that the whole kidnaping incident might have soon been forgotten had it not been for a young second lieutenant. History might have told a different story if Lieutenant George Bascom had not come one day to Fort Buchanan.

Lieutenant Bascom was young and inexperienced. Just out of West Point, he had never been in battle. He didn't know anything about Indians or their ways — indeed, he had never even seen an Indian.

Colonel Morrison explained carefully to Lieutenant Bascom that Cochise and his tribe had been at peace with the Americans for five years. Bascom was to find out if Cochise's people had really kidnaped

101

the child, as John Ward claimed. If Bascom was sure that Cochise was guilty, he was to try and peacefully work out some plan with the chief to get the boy back.

He gave Bascom fifty-four mounted men and an interpreter who spoke Apache. John Ward insisted on going with him.

It was Bascom's first command. He knew nothing about Indians but what he had heard. And what he heard were only tales of ignorance and cruelty.

Now all day on the trail and every night by the campfire, Ward spoke of his own hatred of Indians. He convinced Bascom that Cochise had taken his boy.

After four days of riding through desert and mountains and canyons, they came to the mail station at Apache Pass. Apache Pass was an important stop on the mail route which linked the East to the West. Directly above, in the mountains, lay Cochise's village.

It was clear at a glance that this was a peaceful place. Apache children were playing happily. Some of the Chiricahua Apaches were cutting wood and hay for the people at the mail station. And close to the mail station were the huts in which some of the Indians lived. There were no soldiers.

Lieutenant Bascom sent word to Cochise that he wanted to meet with him under a white flag — the symbol of peace.

His arrival was no surprise to Cochise. For some

time, his scouts had been following every step of Bascom's approach.

Cochise came down the mountain. With him came his wife and son, his brother and two of his brother's sons. No one was armed. Cochise had only his hunting knife which he used every day.

Bascom had put up his tent some distance from the station. Above the tent flew the white flag.

Cochise saw the soldiers standing around the tent, but the white flag promised safety so he paid them no heed. He led his people inside and the Indians sat on the ground and waited in silence.

Those who knew Apache ways understood that the silence was considered good manners. Silence let the other person get used to a new presence, gave them time to think.

Bascom knew so little about Indians that he was startled to see a chief without paint or feathers. Cochise must have wondered what business the young white soldier had with him and why there was not a man to deal with a man!

The young lieutenant began to speak of the raid on Ward's ranch, of the stolen horses and cattle, of the kidnaped boy.

When the words were translated, Cochise wondered what they had to do with him or his tribe.

It was then that Bascom accused Cochise of having stolen the boy and the cattle and he demanded that they be returned at once.

Cochise sat stunned. He held back his anger and

for a long while he was silent, trying to stay calm.

He would explain the situation to this young man and he must do it slowly and carefully as he would explain it to a child. Slowly Cochise explained that for more than five years his people had been at peace and had not killed any white man or taken anything that belonged to them. Instead, they had helped the wagons and mail coaches pass safely through the land. They had even killed Indians from other tribes who attacked the white travelers, in order to keep this peace.

Bascom looked at Ward. Ward insisted Cochise was lying, that he had taken the boy and cattle.

Cochise fought to control his rage.

"I know nothing about this boy or the animals," he said. "Tell me what the boy looks like and my people may be able to help you find him. Other tribes are at war with the whites. Perhaps this was done by the Pinal Apaches or the Coyotero Apaches or the White Mountain Apaches. I will send my warriors to the tribes and they will try to get the boy back. I will . . ."

"You have the boy," Bascom cried. "You are lying, Cochise."

Lying! No man had ever said that word to him.

"And until you return what you have stolen," Bascom continued, "you and your people will be my prisoners. Seize them!"

A wild cry filled the tent. A knife glittered. Cochise jumped to his feet and was across the tent in an instant. "Follow me!" he cried to his people. In seconds, he slashed open the canvas wall with his knife and leaping through the tent, he began to run.

Cochise had taken the guards completely by surprise. When they realized what had happened, they began to shoot. One bullet hit Cochise and as he ran up the steep hill, blood flowed from his wounded leg.

One of the soldiers knocked Cochise's wife to the ground with the end of his gun. One of his brother's sons was stabbed in the stomach with a bayonet. His brother and son — and Cochise's own son were seized.

Only Cochise escaped.

3 Cochise's Pledge

Cochise made his way back to the hills, where his warriors were waiting. Together they rode down to the station.

His plan was to take as captives the three white men who were at the station. He would hold them only long enough to ask for an exchange of prisoners. As soon as he got his family back, the three white men would be set free.

But it was not to be that simple.

It was easy enough to capture the three men at the station. They had always been friendly with Cochise and his people. They had not yet heard what had taken place inside Bascom's tent.

So they walked out, unarmed, to greet the Indians. Cochise's men seized them immediately. Two of the men struggled free and ran toward the stone wall behind the station. Before Cochise could stop him, a warrior fired and one of the white men fell dead.

Just at that moment, some of Lieutenant Bascom's

men were on their way back to the station. They heard the shooting.

One of the soldiers saw a man climbing over the stone wall. He fired — not at an Indian as he supposed, but at one of the escaping white men.

Meanwhile, the Indians took their one remaining captive back to their mountain fortress.

Immediately Cochise ordered his men to ride to Apache Pass. "Stop the stagecoach and the wagon trains going through. Bring me white prisoners. Make sure they are alive and unhurt."

Before the day was done his men returned with two captured white men.

The next morning, Cochise and twenty warriors rode out of the forest. With them was the prisoner they had captured at the station, a man called Wallace. Cochise's plan was to have Wallace speak to Bascom and explain what he wanted — an exchange of prisoners.

The Chiricahuas tied Wallace to the end of a long rope so he could get close enough to Bascom to be heard.

"Bascom!" Wallace called, fear in his voice. "Cochise is holding two more white men. He'll trade the three of us for the Indians."

Bascom's voice was cool. "Tell him he'll get his Indians when we get the Ward boy and the cattle."

Wallace tried to convince Bascom that Cochise did not have the boy. But the young second lieutenant walked back to the station without another word.

The next day, Cochise tried again.

This time, Wallace's voice was shaking. "Bascom," he cried, "let the Indian prisoners go or you'll start a war!"

"When Cochise gives up the Ward boy he'll get his Indians and not before," Bascom replied.

This impossible request again! How could Cochise return what he had not taken!

Day after day Wallace pleaded with Bascom but Bascom refused to change his mind.

Meanwhile, in the dark storeroom of the station, Cochise's family huddled together. Cochise's wife tried to comfort her young son. The boy tried to act like a man. Cochise's brother's son was slowly dying of the bayonet wound he had received.

Cochise's warriors clamored for war. Cochise wondered how much longer he could hold them back.

But he was determined to try to save the peace — at least once more.

Once more Cochise and his warriors came down from the mountain, but this time more than a hundred warriors lined the ridge. Their faces were streaked with war paint and each man held a weapon. Cochise sat tall and erect on his war pony, wearing in his headband the eagle plumes of warfare.

Once again Wallace stumbled down the stony hill, once again tied to the long rope. His voice was hoarse and he could hardly talk. "Listen, Bascom," he whispered. "This is the last time Cochise will

An Apache warrior attacking a covered wagon. A painting by Frederic Remington. The artist lived with cowboys and Indians, and his paintings capture the action of the Wild West.

make his offer to trade us for his people. For the love of God, free the Indians so we may go free. Don't you see this is the end? Don't you see Cochise hasn't got the boy?"

Unmoved, Bascom said again, "When the Ward boy is returned, the Indians will go free."

"Please!" Wallace whispered.

Cochise did not need to have the words translated. He saw Bascom's stubborn face, saw hope dying in Wallace's eyes.

He gave an order. The Chiricahuas rode back into the hills with their captives. They killed the three white men and left their bodies to rot.

Later the soldiers found the bodies. They rode back at once to the depot. They released Cochise's wife and son, and they hanged the rest of Cochise's family.

When scouts brought Cochise the news, he mounted his swiftest pony and rode down the mountain. He saw, hanging from a tree, the bodies of his relatives along with three other Indians that had been captured. He forced himself to gaze at the bodies for a long, long time. Then he cut them down and brought them back to his village.

The wives of his brother and his brother's sons lay down and beat the earth. They painted the dead men's faces and dressed them in their finest clothes so that they would look their best for the long journey to the gods. Then they burned their wickiups and killed their horses and cattle. Everything the dead men had owned was thrown into the flames.

They covered their heads and the heads of their children with black shawls and went far from the village to mourn.

For twenty days, Cochise mourned with them.

On the twenty-first day, a fire was lighted.

The medicine man threw powder into the fire.

Great clouds of black smoke spiraled upward. Cochise raised his arms and lifted his face to the sky.

"There will be war to the end with the White-eyes," he said, using the most hated word for the white man. "For every Apache killed, ten White-eyes will lose their lives. This I swear. This I pledge."

Then for the first time in five years, the war cries of Cochise's tribe rang through the canyons and echoed in the mountains.

4 War!

L IEUTENANT BASCOM had unleashed a war of fury.

Cochise knew that the enemy forces were far greater than the Indian's. It was as if a single tree tried to fight a forest. He knew that the different Apache tribes must join together to fight their enemy.

And so, for the first time in many years, Apache tribes stopped warring among themselves. Apache war chiefs from near and far now gathered in Cochise's stronghold.

One of the older chiefs was Cochise's friend, Mangas Coloradas. The Americans called him Red Sleeves. Sixty-five-year-old Mangas had been fighting for many years, ever since some miners tied him up and beat him — as a warning to stay away from their camp.

The Apache war chiefs planned their strategy well. As a single army, under Cochise, the Apache Nation rode to battle.

From the canyons, the mountains, the deserts of the great Southwest, their war cries rang out.

From a dozen different places, they made their lightning attacks. Ranches and villages were burned and settlers driven from their homes. Mines were destroyed and miners fled for their lives. No white man dared travel through Apache Pass, and the stage line was abandoned.

Cochise had been at war only two months when two thousand miles away — at Fort Sumter in South Carolina — a burst of cannon marked the start of the American Civil War.

Cochise had no way of knowing about this war that threatened to tear the United States apart, but he soon felt its influence. The army needed all of its men. Soldiers were ordered to leave their Southwestern posts and to burn their forts behind them.

Scouts hurried to tell Cochise that the forts were in flames and the soldiers were fleeing. Some Apaches thought this was a sign of their victory. Cochise was wise enough to know otherwise.

They had not yet done battle with the soldiers and had not attacked their forts. Their leaving could have nothing to do with the Apaches.

Now, with the soldiers gone, the Apache raids reached farther and farther — even to the booming town of Tucson. Tucson had been one of the most rapidly growing towns in the Southwest. Now the people fled to California and soon there were only two hundred people left.

In 1865, the Civil War was over but the Apache War went on — a war that Cochise did not choose or want.

Soon soldiers returned to the Southwest. They had their orders from the United States government. The orders were to kill Apache men and take Apache women and children prisoners. Within a year, two thousand Indian women and children had been captured. In that same year — 1866 — one county in the Arizona Territory was still offering $250 for every Apache scalp brought in.

No one thought it was wrong to kill Apaches or seemed to care how it was done.

One day, Cochise's old friend, Mangas Coloradas, was invited to a council of peace by a Colonel West.

Micky Free, as an adult. Kidnaped by the Pinal Apaches as a child, he later became a scout for the U.S. Army.

As Mangas slept by the fire, Colonel West said to the two guards: "That old murderer has left a trail of blood five hundred miles along the old stage line. *I want him dead!*"

One of the guards heated his bayonet in the fire. He plunged the hot bayonet into Mangas' leg. The chief jumped up in pain, and was immediately shot to death.

It was not always easy for the soldiers to find the Apaches. Under Cochise's command, the Apaches were an army of ghosts. They struck — they vanished — they struck again.

They rode their war ponies with speed. They could ride bareback a hundred miles in a single day, on narrow mountain and desert trails known only to them. The soldiers had to stay on the main road. They were slowed down by the heavy packs of equipment their mules carried.

The Apaches rode in silence, using as signals the bark of the fox, the call of the bird, the cry of the coyote. The clink of the soldier's spurs and their rifle-shot signals made their whereabouts known.

The Apaches could get food and drink from the cactus and could ride for many hours without rest. The soldiers had to stop often and make camp.

The United States government spent millions of dollars and sent streams of soldiers to wipe out the Apaches. But Cochise — sometimes with fewer than two hundred warriors — defeated the army again and again.

5 A Man to Trust

THOMAS JONATHAN JEFFORDS had done many daring things in his thirty years of life. He had been captain of a river boat on the Mississippi River, prospected for gold in Indian country, and scouted for the government during the Civil War.

Now in Tucson, he held an almost impossible job. He had to see that the mail got through Apache country. He hired the most reckless riders, armed them with the best rifles, mounted them on the fastest horses, and paid them more money than anyone had before. But rider after rider was killed. In fifteen months, Jeffords lost twenty-two men.

It seemed hopeless to try to get the mail through.

But Tom Jeffords had a plan.

He would seek out Cochise and make a private peace with him. He had heard from many men that for seven years no white man had seen Cochise and lived to tell of it. But he remembered hearing that

Cochise was an honest and brave man who admired honesty and bravery in others.

Jeffords worked for months to learn Apache language and Apache ways. He learned to separate the lies from the truth told about Cochise. Then he asked a friendly Apache boy living near Tucson to show him the way to Cochise's camp. The boy was startled but he agreed to help. Without telling anyone else, the two set out.

After riding some distance, the boy said he must turn back. "An Apache who rides with a white man is not safe from here on," he said.

The boy turned back to Tucson and Jeffords was alone in Apache country — alone with the silence of the land, alone with the trees and the rocks, where perhaps right at that moment an Apache was hiding with a rifle in his hand.

Tom Jeffords built small fires and sent up smoke signals which he knew could be seen for many miles. The smoke signals said he traveled alone and in peace. Jeffords knew his only hope in reaching Cochise alive was to travel openly and boldly, to arouse Cochise's curiosity and not to show fear.

Cochise was indeed curious. He gave orders to his warriors not to harm the white man, but to watch him carefully.

For hours, Jeffords climbed the rough, mountainous country. Apache eyes watched his every move.

Then suddenly, he was in Cochise's camp, surrounded by Apaches. Behind the circle of Apaches,

Jeffords saw a tall, older man and knew this was Cochise.

Jeffords got off his horse as calmly as he could. He knew that if he showed fear, all would be lost. He handed his weapons — rifle, knife, revolver — to an Indian woman, then he said in perfect Apache, "Hold these for me until I leave."

He walked up to Cochise and stood silently before him, as was the Apache way. His heart was pounding but he kept his face calm. After a long while, Jeffords spoke. "I am not at war with Cochise nor do I want to be." He told Cochise why he had come and what he wanted.

For a long time Cochise looked at this white man, with his strange red beard and his honest eyes. Then he motioned Jeffords to follow him to his wickiup.

The two men talked long into the night. They

talked about many things. Jeffords told Cochise about his country and his president and why his people were coming now to Apache country, why it was important for the United States to have Apache Pass open, so that settlers could travel westward. He told about the mail riders who had been killed though they came not to make war but to carry the mail through.

Cochise spoke of the years in which Apaches too had been in peace but had been killed, and how he had kept the white men safe from other tribes.

Cochise told Jeffords many stories of how the white men betrayed the Apaches and how his friend, Mangas Coloradas, had been killed. Jeffords did not try to make excuses for the white man's behavior. Cochise respected him even more for this.

Cochise discovered that he liked this white man and even felt he could trust him. Jefford's admiration for the great chief also grew with every passing hour.

The following day, Cochise said, "Your riders can pass safely through these mountains. And you, *Taglito*, are my friend and will always be welcomed here."

Jeffords smiled at the Apache word for red-beard. *Taglito*. He liked the name.

Cochise kept his word as Jeffords knew he would. Though the war went on and the white men and the Apaches continued to fight, Jeffords' riders carried the mail safely through Apache Pass.

In the months that followed, Jeffords came often to Cochise's camp and the friendship between the two men grew stronger.

They talked of war and they talked of peace. No longer were there four thousand Apache warriors united in fighting the enemy. By now the greater part of the Apache Nation had been defeated in battle and those who survived had been sent to live on reservations.

In Cochise's band there were fewer than three hundred people. But Cochise did not surrender. He had been told what had happened to the Apache tribes who had put down their arms and now lived on reservations. Soldiers guarded them day and night. The white men in charge of the Indian's welfare — the Indian agents — took the food that was meant for the Indians.

General George Crook reported, "I have never yet seen an Indian who was not an example of honor compared to the wretches who plunder him of the little our government gives him."

Cochise and Jeffords spoke of what had happened to the Aravaipa Apache Nation. They had gone to Camp Grant near Tucson, wishing to make peace with the army. The army put them up in huts overnight. Before dawn, a mob from Tucson attacked them. They went from hut to hut clubbing the sleeping Indians to death.

Horrified by the crime, Americans across the nation were outraged. President Grant wrote to the

General Oliver Otis Howard, called the Christian General.

Ulysses S. Grant, 18th President of the United States.

governor: "Bring the guilty to trial." One hundred and four Americans, Mexicans, and Papago Indians, deadly enemies of the Apaches, were charged with the murders. The jury declared them not guilty.

The massacre at Camp Grant had made many more Americans aware of the cruelty with which the Indians were being treated. President Grant was now more anxious than ever to end the Apache War. In ten years, the war had cost the U.S. government one thousand lives and forty million dollars.

Now the government spoke of a policy of kindness and firmness and peace. But it was not enough for Grant to speak of such a policy. He had to convince Cochise that he meant it.

In the fall of 1871, President Grant sent a special soldier to Arizona, one whom he believed could make peace with Cochise.

That man was General Oliver Otis Howard. Many men called him the "Christian General." He kept his

Bible with him always and he read from it every day. With his flowing white hair and beard, he looked as if he might have stepped out of the Bible.

As soon as General Howard arrived in Arizona, he sought out Jeffords, the one man, he had been told, who could lead him to Cochise.

"What powers do you have, sir?" Jeffords asked him.

"President Grant has given me full powers to make any settlement I think is right," General Howard replied.

"If I take you to Cochise, will you go without soldiers and weapons?" Jeffords asked.

General Howard did not hesitate. "If that is the only way, yes! I'd like to take along my aide, Captain Sladen, if that is all right. You are in command, Mr. Jeffords. I will follow your orders."

Jeffords felt a hope he had not experienced in years, a hope that this man might very well be the one to end eleven terrible years of war.

The journey to Cochise's mountains took many days. On the way, General Howard asked many questions. Jeffords told the general that Cochise was an honorable man and if he gave his word he would keep it. Jeffords spoke of Cochise's dignity and honesty and how his people followed him as they would a king. He said that few white men had tried to understand him and that if only Lieutenant Bascom had, this war would not have started in the first place.

The miner rinsed away soil from his pan. "Gold! We're rich, boys!"

Several Chiricahua Indians joined them on their way. One day they passed through a settlement of gold miners. The miners blocked their path, shouting, "Apache murderers! Kill 'em!" Quickly General Howard stepped between the miners and the Indians. In a calm, firm voice, he said, "If any killing is done, you must kill me first." The crowd fell back and Howard led his party on.

6 Peace with Honor

FINALLY, General Howard and the Chiricahuas reached Cochise's camp.

Cochise met General Howard with great dignity. Jeffords explained to Cochise why the general had come.

"Can he be trusted?" Cochise asked his friend.

Jeffords answered with caution and honesty. "I do not know but I believe so."

"Will he do what he says he will?" Cochise asked.

"I do not know," Jeffords said, "but I think he will."

Cochise and Howard talked and Jeffords translated. Cochise told about the peace he had made long ago and how he had protected the travelers in Apache Pass.

He told how he had promised peace and how he had kept his promise. Then he told the story of Lieutenant Bascom and the treachery under the white flag.

When his story was told, he asked the general how long he would stay.

"As long as it takes to make peace with you," the general replied. "I would like you to move all of your people to good fertile land on the Rio Grande River. There your people will have all the land they need."

"No!" Cochise said. "No, we will not be moved to any reservation. Our home is here, where our fathers' homes have been. Our roots go deep here. Like the great trees you see all around you, our roots cannot be pulled from the earth."

"Then perhaps this land can be your reservation," General Howard suggested.

Cochise took Howard to a high ridge which overlooked the land. The general could see why Cochise and his people could not leave the land — its mountains, forests, streams, and canyons. The setting sun warmed the clay, cliff walls, deepened the greens of the forests, and tinted the mountain ranges purple.

In the days that followed, Cochise named his terms. His people must be allowed to keep their weapons. They were not a conquered nation and they were not surrendering. They were making peace as free men. And they did not want any thieving Indian agents. "I want a man I can trust to deal with the Americans," Cochise said. "I want Taglito."

Jeffords stopped translating. He jumped up in surprise. "I do not want to be an Indian agent," he said.

Cochise said, "Then there is no need of further talk."

"You must understand that there will not be peace

Taza, oldest son of Cochise.

if you refuse," General Howard said to Jeffords. "I will see to it that you will receive your authority direct from the President."

Jeffords looked at his Apache friend and thought how important this peace would be.

He sighed and said at last, "I will take the job."

Cochise agreed to call his people to a council of

peace. He said that it would be many days before they could all come together, for many were out on hunts and raids.

While waiting for the warriors to return, General Howard and Cochise talked often, and Howard's admiration for the chief grew every day. Often he thought, "The United States could use more men like Cochise, with his honor and his military genius."

The general kept a diary of his days in Cochise's mountains and while he wrote, the children gathered around him. Howard taught Cochise's youngest son how to write his name in English. Sometimes the general would rest on a blanket out of doors and the children would lie down next to him.

Their raids and hunts over, Cochise's warriors slowly drifted into the camp. When they had all gathered, Cochise took them to the council grounds and the white men were asked to stay behind until they were called for.

For five days Jeffords and Howard waited.

When at last they were asked to join the council, Howard thought he had never before seen such an impressive sight. The warriors were seated in a circle and around them, in a larger circle, were the women. Cochise stood in the center, his face lifted to the sky.

"A few of our warriors have refused to follow this peace," he said. "From this day forward they will not be welcome here. All the others will follow me in peace."

And as long as both Cochise and Jeffords lived, peace was kept between the Americans and the Chiricahua Apaches.

Cochise died in 1874. He did not live to see the final fate of his people. For the promise made by Howard was broken and they were driven out of their mountain home and moved to a distant reservation.

High in the Arizona mountains where the Chiricahua Apaches had lived, there is a mountain peak which appears to be a rugged profile. It is called Cochise Mountain.

Somewhere near here, Cochise is buried. The only white man who knew exactly where was Tom Jeffords. And he kept the secret.